Fires

Book 2

The Ovens, And Other Tales

By

Wilfrid Wilson Gibson

Double 9 BOOKS

Fires
Book 2
The Ovens, And Other Tales
by Wilfrid Wilson Gibson

ISBN: 978-93-61421-40-2

Published by

DOUBLE 9 BOOKS

2/13-B, Ansari Road
Daryaganj, New Delhi – 110002
info@double9books.com
www.double9books.com
Tel. 011-40042856

ABOUT THE AUTHOR

Wilfrid Wilson Gibson, a notable English poet of the early 20th century, left an indelible mark on literature with his profound insights into the human condition. Born in 1878, Gibson's works often explored themes of nature, social injustice, and the struggles of the working class. Among his notable works, "Fires: The Stone, and Other Tales" stands out as a masterpiece of poetry and prose. In "Fires," Gibson presents a collection of poignant tales that delve into the complexities of life, each story serving as a metaphorical flame illuminating the human experience. The subtitle, "The Stone, and Other Tales," hints at the varied subjects explored within the book, from the enduring resilience of the human spirit to the harsh realities of existence. Gibson's mastery lies in his ability to weave together lyrical language with profound insights, creating a tapestry of emotion and imagery that resonates deeply with readers. Through his stories, he invites readers to confront universal truths and contemplate the intricacies of the human condition. "Fires: The Stone, and Other Tales" stands as a testament to Gibson's literary talent and his ability to capture the essence of life in all its beauty and complexity. With its evocative prose and timeless themes, this masterpiece continues to inspire and move readers around the world.

CONTENTS

THE CRANE

The biggest crane on earth, it lifts
Two hundred ton more easily
Than I can lift my heavy head:
And when it swings, the whole world shifts,
Or so, at least, it seems to me,
As, day and night, adream I lie
Upon my crippled back in bed,
And watch it up against the sky.

My mother, hunching in her chair,
Day-long, and stitching trousers there--
At three-and-three the dozen pair...
She'd sit all night, and stitch for me,
Her son, if I could only wear...
She never lifts her eyes to see
The big crane swinging through the air.

But, though she has no time to talk,
She always cleans the window-pane,
That I may see it, clear and plain:
And, as I watch it move, I walk
Who never walked in all my days...
And, often, as I dream agaze,
I'm up and out: and it is I
Who swing the crane across the sky.
Right up above the wharf I stand,
And touch a lever with my hand,
To lift a bunch of girders high,

A truck of coal, a field of grain
In sacks, a bundle of big trees,
Or beasts, too frightened in my grip
To wonder at their skiey trip:
And then I let the long arm dip
Without a hitch, without a slip,
To set them safely in the ship
That waits to take them overseas.

My mother little dreams it's I,
Up there, as tiny as a fly,
Who stand above the biggest crane,
And swing the ship-loads through the sky;
While she sits, hunching in her chair,
Day-long, and stitching trousers there--
At three-and-three the dozen pair.

And sometimes when it turns me dizzy,
I lie and watch her, ever busy;
And wonder at a lot of things
I never speak to her about:
I wonder why she never sings
Like other people on the stair...
And why, whenever she goes out
Upon a windy day, the air
Makes her sad eyes so strangely bright...
And if the colour of her hair
Was brown like mine, or always white...
And why, when through the noise of feet
Of people passing in the street,
She hears a dog yelp or sheep bleat,
She always starts up in her chair,
And looks before her with strange stare,
Yet, seeing nothing anywhere:
Though, right before her, through the sky,

The biggest crane goes swinging by.

But, it's a lucky day and rare
When she's the time to talk with me...
Though, only yesterday, when night
Shut out, at last, the crane from sight...
She, in her bed, and thinking I
Was sleeping--though I watch the sky,
At times, till it is morning-light,
And ships are waiting to unload--
I heard her murmur drowsily:
"The pit-pat-pattering of feet,
All night, along the moonlit road...
A yelp, a whistle, and a bleat...
The bracken's deep and soft and dry...
And safe and snug, and no one near...
The little burn sings low and sweet,
The little burn sings shrill and clear...
And loud all night the cock-grouse talks...
There's naught in heaven or earth to fear...
The pit-pat-pattering of feet...
A yelp, a whistle, and a bleat..."
And then, she started up in bed:
I felt her staring, as she said:
"I wonder if he ever hears
The pit-pat-pattering of sheep,
Or smells the broken bracken stalks...
While she is lying sound-asleep
Beside him ... after all these years--
Just nineteen years, this very night--
Remembering? ... and now, his son,
A man ... and never stood upright!"

And then, I heard a sound of tears;
But dared not speak, or let her know

I'd caught a single whisper, though
I wondered long what she had done
That she should fear the pattering feet:
And when those queer words in the night
Had fretted me half-dead with fright,
And set my throbbing head abeat...
Out of the darkness, suddenly,
The crane's long arm swung over me,
Among the stars, high overhead...
And then it dipped, and clutched my bed
And I had not a breath to cry,
Before it swung me through the sky,
Above the sleeping city high,
Where blinding stars went blazing by...

My mother, hunching in her chair,
Day-long, and stitching trousers there,
At three-and-three the dozen pair,
With quiet eyes and smooth white hair...
You'd little think a yelp or bleat
Could start her; or that she was weeping
So sorely, when she thought me sleeping.
She never tells me why she fears
The pit-pat-pattering of feet
All night along the moonlit road...
Or what's the wrong that she has done...
I wonder if 'twould bring her tears,
If she could know that I, her son--
A man, who never stood upright,
But all the livelong day must lie,
And watch, beyond the window-pane
The swaying of the biggest crane--
That I, within its clutch, last night,
Went whirling through the starry sky.

THE LIGHTHOUSE

Just as my watch was done, the fog had lifted;
And we could see the flashing of our light;
And see, once more, the reef beyond the Head,
O'er which, six days and nights, the mist had drifted--
Six days and nights in thick white mist had drifted,
Until it seemed all time to mist had drifted,
And day and night were but one blind white night.

But on the seventh midnight the wind shifted:
And I was glad to tumble into bed,
Thankful to hear no more the blaring horn,
That ceaselessly had sounded, night and morn,
With moaning echoes through the mist, to warn
The blind, bewildered ships at sea:
Yet, though as tired as any dog,
I lay awhile, and seemed to feel
Fog lying on my eyes still heavily;
And still, the horn unceasingly
Sang through my head, till gradually
Through night's strange stillness, over me
Sweet sleep began to steal,
Sleep, blind and thick and fleecy as the fog.

For all I knew, I might have slept
A moment, or eternity;
When, startled by a crash,
I waked to find I'd leapt
Upright on the floor:
And stood there, listening to the smash

Of falling glass ... and then a thud
Of something heavy tumbling
Into the next room...
A pad of naked feet...
A moan ... a sound of stumbling ...
A heavier thud ... and then no more.
And I stood shivering in the gloom,
With creeping flesh, and tingling blood,
Until I gave myself a shake
To bring my wits more wide awake;
And lit a lantern, and flung wide the door.
Half-dazed, and dazzled by the light,
At first it seemed I'd only find
A broken pane, a flapping blind:
But when I raised the lantern o'er my head,
I saw a naked boy upon the bed,
Who crouched and shuddered on the folded sheet;
And, on his face, before my feet,
A naked man, who lay as if quite dead,
Though on his broken knuckles blood was red:
And all my wits awakened at the sight.

I set the lantern down; and took the child,
Who looked at me, with piteous eyes and wild;
And chafed his chill, wet body, till it glowed;
And forcing spirit 'twixt his chattering teeth,
I tucked him snugly in beneath
The blankets, and soon left him warmly stowed:
And stooped to tend the man, who lay
Still senseless on the floor.

I turned him off his face;
And laid him on the other bed;
And washed and staunched his wound.
And yet for all that I could do,

I could not bring him to,
Or see a trace
Of life returning to that heavy head.

It seemed he'd swooned,
When through the window he'd made way,
Just having strength to lay
The boy in safety. Still as death,
He lay, without a breath:
And seeing I could do no more
To help him in the fight for life;
I turned again to tend the lad;
And, as I looked on him, was glad
To find him sleeping quietly.

So, fetching fuel, I lit a fire:
And quickly had as big a blaze
As any housewife could desire:
Then, 'twixt the beds, I set a chair,
That I might watch until they stirred:
And as I saw them lying there--
The sleeping boy, and him who lay
In that strange stiller sleep, 'twas plain
That they were son and father, now
I'd time to look, and wonder how,
In such a desperate plight,
Without a stitch or rag,
They'd taken refuge from the night.
And, as I wondered drowsily,
It seemed yet queerer and more queer;
For round the Head the rocks are sheer,
With scarce a foothold for a bird;
And it seemed quite beyond belief
That any wrecked upon the reef,
Could swim ashore, and scale the crag,

By daylight, let alone by night

But, they who live beside the sea
Know naught's too wonderful to be:
And, as I sat, and heard
The quiet breathing of the child,
Great weariness came over me;
And, in a kind of daze,
I watched the blaze,
With nodding head:
And must have slept, for, presently,
I found the man was sitting up in bed:
And talking to himself, with wide, unseeing eyes.
At first, I hardly made out what he said:
But soon his voice, so hoarse and wild,
Grew calm: and, straining, I could hear
The broken words, that came with many sighs.

"Yes, lad: she's going: but, there's naught to fear:
For I can swim: and tow you in the belt.
Come, let's join hands together; and leap clear...
Aye, son: it's dark and cold ... but you have felt
The cold and dark before...
And you should scorn...
And we must be near shore...
For, hark the horn!
Think of your mother, and your home, and leap...
She thinks of us, lad, waking or asleep...
You would not leave her lonely?
Nay! ... then ... go! ...
Well done, lad! ... Nay! I'm here...
Aye, son, it's cold: but you're too big to fear.
Now then, you're snug: I've got you safe in tow:
The worst is over: and we've only
To make for land ... we've naught ... to do ... but steer...

But steer ... but steer..."

He paused; and sank down in the bed, quite done:
And lay a moment silent, while his son
Still slumbered in the other bed,
And on his quiet face the firelight shone.
Then, once again, the father raised his head,
And rambled on...
"Say, lad, what cheer?
I thought you'd dropped asleep: but you're all right.
We'll rest a moment ... I'm quite out of breath...
It's further than ... Nay, son! there's naught to fear...
The land must be quite near...
The horn is loud enough!
Aye, lad, it's cold:
But, you're too old
To cry for cold.
Now ... keep ... tight hold:
And we'll be off again.
I've got my breath..."

He sank, once more, as still as death,
With hands that clutched the counterpane:
But still the boy was sleeping quietly.
And then, the father sat up suddenly:
And cried: "See! See!
The land! the land!
It's near ... I touch it with my hand."
And now, "Oh God!" he moaned.
Small wonder, when he saw what lay before--
The black, unbroken crags, so grim and high,
That must have seemed to him to soar
Sheer from the sea's edge to the sky.
But, soon, he plucked up heart, once more:
"We're safe, lad--safe ashore!

A narrow ledge, but land, firm land.
We'll soon be high and dry.
Nay, son: we can't stay here:
The waves would have us back;
Or we should perish of the cold.
Come, lad: there's naught to fear...
You must be brave and bold.
Perhaps, we'll strike a track.
Aye, son: it's steep, and black,
And slimy to the hold:
But we must climb, and see! the mist is gone.
The stars are shining clear...
Think, son, your mother's at the top;
And you'll be up in no time. See, that star,
The brightest star that ever shone,
Just think it's she who watches you;
And knows that you'll be brave and true.
Come, lad: we may not stop...
Or, else, the cold...
Give me your hand...
Your foot there, now ... just room to stand.
It cannot be so far...
We'll soon be up ... this work should make us warm.
Thank God, it's not a storm,
Or we should scarce ... your foot, here, firm...
Nay, lad! you must not squirm.
Come, be a man: you shall not fall:
I'll hold you tight.
There: now, you are my own son, after all!
Your mother, lad,
Her star burns bright...
And we're already half-way up the height...
Your mother will be glad,
Aye, she'll be glad to hear

Of her brave boy who had no fear.

Your foot ... your hand ... 'twas but a bird
You startled out of bed:
'Twould think it queer
To wake up, suddenly, and see your head!
And, when you stirred...
Nay! steady, lad!
Or you will send your dad...
Your hand ... your foot ... we'll rest upon this ledge...
Why, son, we're at the top! I feel the edge,
And grass, soft, dewy grass!
Let go, one moment; and I'll draw you up...
Now, lad! ... Thank God! that's past...
And you are safe, at last:
You're safe, you're safe ... and now, my precious lass
Will see her son, her little son, again.

I never thought to reach the top, to-night.
God! What a height!
Nay! but you must not look: 'twould turn your head
And we must not stand shivering here...
And see ... a flashing light...
It's sweeping towards us: and now you stand bright.
Ah, your poor, bleeding hands and feet!
My little son, my sweet!
There's nothing more to fear.
A lighthouse, lad! And we must make for it.
You're tired; I'll carry you a bit.
Nay, son: 'twill warm me up...
And there will be a fire and bed;
And ev'n perhaps a cup
Of something hot to drink,
And something good to eat.
And think, son, only think,

Your home ... and mother ... once again."

Once more, the weary head
Sank back upon the bed:
And, for a while, he hardly stirred;
But only muttered, now and then,
A broken word,
As though to cheer
His son, who still slept quietly,
Upon the other side of me.

And then, my blood ran cold to hear
A sudden cry of fear:
"My son! My son!
Ah, God, he's done!
I thought I'd laid him on the bed...
I've laid him on white mist, instead:
He's fallen sheer..."

Then, I sprang up; and cried: "Your son is here!"
And, taking up the sleeping boy,
I bore him to his father's arms:
And, as he nestled to his breast,
Kind life came back to those wild eyes;
And filled them with deep joy:
And, free of all alarms,
The son and father lay,
Together, in sweet rest,
While through the window stole the strange, clear light of
day.

THE MONEY

They found her cold upon the bed.
The cause of death, the doctor said,
Was nothing save the lack of bread.

Her clothes were but a sorry rag
That barely hid the nakedness
Of her poor body's piteous wreck:
Yet, when they stripped her of her dress,
They found she was not penniless;
For, in a little silken bag,
Tied with red ribbon round her neck,
Was four-pound-seventeen-and-five.

"It seems a strange and shameful thing
That she should starve herself to death,
While she'd the means to keep alive.
Why, such a sum would keep the breath
Within her body till she'd found
A livelihood; and it would bring...
But, there is very little doubt
She'd set her heart upon a grand
And foolish funeral--for the pride
Of poor folk, who can understand!--
And so, because she was too proud
To meet death penniless, she died."

And talking, talking, they trooped out:
And, as they went, I turned about
To look upon her in her shroud;
And saw again the quiet face

That filled with light that shameful place,
Touched with the tender, youthful grace
Death brings the broken and outworn
To comfort kind hearts left to mourn.

And as I stood, the sum they'd found
Rang with a queer, familiar ring
Of some uncouth, uncanny sound
Heard in dark ages underground;
And "four-pound-seventeen-and-five"
Through all my body seemed to sing,
Without recalling anything
To help me, strive as I might strive.

But, as I stumbled down the stairs
Into the alley's gloom and stench--
A whiff of burning oil
That took me unawares--
And I knew all there was to tell.
And, though the rain in torrents fell,
I walked on, heedless, through the drench
And, all the while, I seemed to sit
Upon a tub in Lansel pit;
And in the candle-light to see
John Askerton, a "deputy,"
Who paused awhile to talk with me,
His kind face glistening black with toil.

"'Twas here I found him dead, beside
His engine. All the other men
Were up--for things were slack just then--
And I'd one foot upon the cage;
When, all at once, I caught the smell
Of burning. Even as I turned
To see what it could be that burned,
The seam behind was choked with stife.

But, as her time drew near,
Her heart was filled with fear:
And when the lilac burst to bloom,
And brought the Summer in a breath,
A presence seemed to fill the room,
And fill her heart with death:
And, as her husband lay asleep,
Beside her, on the bed,
Into her breast the thought would creep
That he was dreaming of the dead.
And all the mother's heart in her
Was mad with mother-jealousy
Of that sweet scented lilac tree;
And, blind with savage ecstasy,
Night after night she lay,
Until the blink of day,
With staring eyes and wild,
Half-crazy, lest the lilac tree
Should come betwixt him and his child.
By day, her mother-tenderness
Was turned to brooding bitterness,
Whene'er she looked upon the bloom:
And, if she slept at all at night,
Her heart would waken in affright
To smell the lilac in the gloom:
And, when it rained, it seemed to her,
The fresh keen scent was bitterer:
Though, when the blaze of morning came,
And flooded all the room,
The perfume burnt her heart like flame.
As, in the dark,
One night she lay,
A dark thought shot
Through her hot heart:
And, from a spark

Of smouldering wrong,
Hate burst to fire.
Now, quaking cold,
Now, quivering hot,
With breath indrawn,
Through time untold,
She 'waited dawn
That lagged too long
For her desire.

And when, at last, at break of day,
Her husband rose, and went his way
About his daily toil,
She, too, arose, and dressed,
With frenzy in her breast;
And stole downstairs, and took a spade,
And digged about the lilac roots,
And laid them bare of soil:
Then, with a jagged blade,
She hacked and slashed the naked roots--
She hacked and slashed with frantic hand,
Until the lilac scarce might stand;
And then again the soil she laid
About the bleeding roots--
(It seemed to her, the sap ran red
About the writhing roots!)
But, now her heart was eased of strife,
Since she had sapped the lilac's life;
And, frenzy-spent, she dropped the knife:
Then, dizzily she crept to bed,
And lay all day as one nigh dead.

That night a sudden storm awoke,
And struck the slumbering earth to life:
And, as the heavens in thunder broke,
She lay exulting in the strife

Of flash and peal,
And gust and rain;
For now, she thought: the lightning-stroke
Will lay the lilac low;
And he need never know
How I ... and then, again,
Her heart went cold with dread,
As she remembered that the knife
Still lay beneath the lilac tree...
A blinding flash,
A lull, a crash,
A rattling peal...
And suddenly,
She felt her senses reel:
And, crying out: "The knife! The knife!"
Her pangs were on her...
Dawn was red,
When she awoke upon the bed
To life--and knew her babe was dead.
She rose: and cried out fearfully:
"The lilac tree! The lilac tree!"
Then fell back in a swoon.

But, when she waked again at noon,
And looked upon her sleeping child;
And laid her hand upon its head,
No more the mother's heart was wild,
For hate and fear were dead;
And all her brooding bitterness
Broke into tears of tenderness.

And, not a word the father said
About the lilac, lying dead.

A week went by, and Whitsuntide
Came round: and, as she lay,
And looked upon the newborn day,

Her husband, lying by her side,
Spoke to her very tenderly:
"Wife, 'tis again our wedding day,
And we will plant a lilac tree
In memory of the babe that died."

They planted a white lilac tree
Upon their wedding day:
And, when the time of blossom came,
With kindly hearts they lay.
The sunlight streamed upon the bed:
The scent of lilac filled the room:
And, as they smelt the breathing bloom,
They thought upon the dead.

THE OLD MAN

The boat put in at dead of night;
And, when I reached the house, 'twas sleeping dark.
I knew my gentlest tap would be a spark
To set my home alight:
My mother ever listening in her sleep
For my returning step, would leap
Awake with welcome; and my father's eyes
Would twinkle merrily to greet me;
And my young sister would run down to meet me
With sleepy sweet surprise.

And yet, awhile, I lingered
Upon the threshold, listening;
And watched the cold stars glistening,
And seemed to hear the deep
Calm breathing of the house asleep--
In easy sleep, so deep, I almost feared to break it;
And, even as I fingered
The knocker, loth to wake it,
Like some uncanny inkling
Of news from otherwhere,
I felt a cold breath in my hair,
As though, with chin upon my shoulder,
One waited hard, upon my heel,
With pricking eyes of steel,
Though well I knew that not a soul was there.

Until, at last, grown bolder,
I rapped; and in a twinkling,
The house was all afire
With welcome in the night:
First, in my mother's room, a light;
And then, her foot upon the stair;
A bolt shot back; a candle's flare:
A happy cry; and to her breast
She hugged her heart's desire:
And hushed her fears to rest.

Then, shivering in the keen night air,
My sleepy sister, laughing came;
And drew us in: and stirred to flame
The smouldering kitchen-fire; and set
The kettle on the kindling red:
And, as I watched the homely blaze,
And thought of wandering days
With sharp regret;
I missed my father: then I heard
How he was still a-bed;
And had been ailing, for a day or so;
But, now was waking, if I'd go...
My foot already on the stair,
In answer to my mother's word
I turned; and saw in dull amaze,
Behind her, as she stood all unaware,
An old man sitting in my father's chair.
A strange old man ... yet, as I looked at him,
Before my eyes, a dim
Remembrance seemed to swim
Of some old man, who'd lurked about the boat,
While we were still at sea;
And who had crouched beside me, at the oar,
As we had rowed ashore;

Though, at the time, I'd taken little note,
I felt I'd seen that strange old man before:
But, how he'd come to follow me,
Unknown...
And to be sitting there...
Then I recalled the cold breath in my hair,
When I had stood, alone,
Before the bolted door.

And now my mother, wondering sore
To see me stare and stare,
So strangely, at an empty chair,
Turned, too; and saw the old man there.

And as she turned, he slowly raised
His drooping head;
And looked upon her with her husband's eyes.
She stood, a moment, dazed;
And watched him slowly rise,
As though to come to her:
Then, with a cry, she sped
Upstairs, ere I could stir.

Still dazed, I let her go, alone:
I heard her footstep overhead:
I heard her drop beside the bed,
With low forsaken moan.

Yet, I could only stare and stare
Upon my father's empty chair.

THE HARE

My hands were hot upon a hare,
Half-strangled, struggling in a snare--
My knuckles at her warm wind-pipe--
When suddenly, her eyes shot back,
Big, fearful, staggering and black:
And, ere I knew, my grip was slack;
And I was clutching empty air,
Half-mad, half-glad at my lost luck...
When I awoke beside the stack.

'Twas just the minute when the snipe,
As though clock-wakened, every jack,
An hour ere dawn, dart in and out
The mist-wreaths filling syke and slack,
And flutter wheeling round about,
And drumming out the Summer night.
I lay star-gazing yet a bit;
Then, chilly-skinned, I sat upright,
To shrug the shivers from my back;
And, drawing out a straw to suck,
My teeth nipped through it at a bite...
The liveliest lad is out of pluck
An hour ere dawn--a tame cock-sparrow--
When cold stars shiver through his marrow,
And wet mist soaks his mother-wit.
But, as the snipe dropped, one by one;
And one by one the stars blinked out;
I knew 'twould only need the sun
To send the shudders right about:

And, as the clear East faded white,
I watched and wearied for the sun--
The jolly, welcome, friendly sun--
The sleepy sluggard of a sun
That still kept snoozing out of sight,
Though well he knew the night was done
And, after all, he caught me dozing,
And leapt up, laughing, in the sky
Just as my lazy eyes were closing:
And it was good as gold to lie
Full-length among the straw, and feel
The day wax warmer every minute,
As, glowing glad, from head to heel,
I soaked and rolled rejoicing in it...
When from the corner of my eye,
Upon a heathery knowe hard-by,
With long lugs cocked, and eyes astare,
Yet all serene, I saw a hare.

Upon my belly in the straw,
I lay, and watched her sleek her fur,
As, daintily, with well-licked paw,
She washed her face and neck and ears:
Then, clean and comely in the sun,
She kicked her heels up, full of fun,
As if she did not care a pin
Though she should jump out of her skin,
And leapt and lolloped, free of fears,
Until my heart frisked round with her.
"And yet, if I but lift my head,
You'll scamper off, young Puss," I said.
"Still, I can't lie, and watch you play,
Upon my belly half-the-day.
The Lord alone knows where I'm going:
But, I had best be getting there.

Last night I loosed you from the snare--
Asleep, or waking, who's for knowing!--
So, I shall thank you now for showing
Which art to take to bring me where
My luck awaits me. When you're ready
To start, I'll follow on your track.
Though slow of foot, I'm sure and steady..."
She pricked her ears, then set them back;
And like a shot was out of sight:
And, with a happy heart and light,
As quickly I was on my feet;
And following the way she went,
Keen as a lurcher on the scent,
Across the heather and the bent,
Across the quaking moss and peat.
Of course, I lost her soon enough,
For moorland tracks are steep and rough;
And hares are made of nimbler stuff
Than any lad of seventeen,
However lanky-legged and tough,
However, kestrel-eyed and keen:
And I'd at last to stop and eat
The little bit of bread and meat
Left in my pocket overnight.
So, in a hollow, snug and green,
I sat beside a burn, and dipped
The dry bread in an icy pool;
And munched a breakfast fresh and cool...
And then sat gaping like a fool...
For, right before my very eyes,
With lugs acock, and eyes astare,
I saw again the selfsame hare.

So, up I jumped, and off she slipped:
And I kept sight of her until

I stumbled in a hole, and tripped;
And came a heavy, headlong spill:
And she, ere I'd the wit to rise,
Was o'er the hill, and out of sight:
And, sore and shaken with the tumbling,
And sicker at my foot for stumbling,
I cursed my luck, and went on, grumbling,
The way her flying heels had fled.

The sky was cloudless overhead;
And just alive with larks asinging:
And, in a twinkling, I was swinging
Across the windy hills, lighthearted.
A kestrel at my footstep started,
Just pouncing on a frightened mouse,
And hung o'erhead with wings a-hover:
Through rustling heath an adder darted:
A hundred rabbits bobbed to cover:
A weasel, sleek and rusty-red,
Popped out of sight as quick as winking:
I saw a grizzled vixen slinking
Behind a clucking brood of grouse
That rose and cackled at my coming:
And all about my way were flying
The peewit, with their slow wings creaking
And little jack-snipe darted, drumming:
And now and then a golden plover
Or redshank piped with reedy whistle.
But never shaken bent or thistle
Betrayed the quarry I was seeking
And not an instant, anywhere
Did I clap eyes upon a hare.

So, travelling still, the twilight caught me:
And as I stumbled on, I muttered:
"A deal of luck the hare has brought me!

The wind and I must spend together
A hungry night among the heather.
If I'd her here..." And as I uttered,
I tripped, and heard a frightened squeal;
And dropped my hands in time to feel
The hare just bolting 'twixt my feet.
She slipped my clutch: and I stood there
And cursed that devil-littered hare,
That left me stranded in the dark
In that wide waste of quaggy peat
Beneath black night without a spark:
When, looking up, I saw a flare
Upon a far-off hill, and said:
"By God, the heather is afire!
It's mischief at this time of year..."
And then, as one bright flame shot higher,
And booths and vans stood out quite clear;
My wits came back into my head:
And I remembered Brough Hill Fair.
And, as I stumbled towards the glare,
I knew the sudden kindling meant
The Fair was over for the day;
And all the cattle-folk away
And gipsy-folk and tinkers now
Were lighting supper-fires without
Each caravan and booth and tent.
And, as I climbed the stiff hill-brow,
I quite forgot my lucky hare.
I'd something else to think about:
For well I knew there's broken meat
For empty bellies after fair-time;
And looked to have a royal rare time
With something rich and prime to eat:
And then to lie and toast my feet
All night beside the biggest fire.

But, even as I neared the first,
A pleasant whiff of stewing burst
From out a smoking pot a-bubble:
And, as I stopped behind the folk
Who sprawled around, and watched it seething
A woman heard my eager breathing,
And, turning, caught my hungry eye:
And called out to me: "Draw in nigher,
Unless you find it too much trouble;
Or you've a nose for better fare,
And go to supper with the Squire...
You've got the hungry parson's air!"
And all looked up, and took the joke,
As I dropped gladly to the ground
Among them, where they all lay gazing
Upon the bubbling and the blazing.
My eyes were dazzled by the fire
At first; and then I glanced around;
And, in those swarthy, fire-lit faces--
Though drowsing in the glare and heat
And snuffing the warm savour in,
Dead-certain of their fill of meat--
I felt the bit between the teeth,
The flying heels, the broken traces,
And heard the highroad ring beneath
The trampling hoofs: and knew them kin.
Then for the first time, standing there
Behind the woman who had hailed me,
I saw a girl with eyes astare
That looked in terror o'er my head:
And, all at once, my courage failed me...
For now again, and sore-adread,
My hands were hot upon a hare,
That struggled, strangling in the snare...
Then once more as the girl stood clear,

Before me--quaking cold with fear
I saw the hare look from her eyes...

And when, at last, I turned to see
What held her scared, I saw a man--
A fat man with dull eyes aleer--
Within the shadow of the van:
And I was on the point to rise
To send him spinning 'mid the wheels,
And twist his neck between his heels,
And stop his leering grin with mud...
And would have done it in a tick...
When, suddenly, alive with fright,
She started, with red, parted lips,
As though she guessed we'd come to grips,
And turned her black eyes full on me...
And, as I looked into their light,
My heart forgot the lust of fight,
And something shot me to the quick,
And ran like wildfire through my blood,
And tingled to my finger-tips...
And, in a dazzling flash, I knew
I'd never been alive before...
And she was mine for evermore.

While all the others slept asnore
In caravan and tent that night,
I lay alone beside the fire;
And stared into its blazing core,
With eyes that would not shut or tire,
Because the best of all was true,
And they looked still into the light
Of her eyes, burning ever bright.
Within the brightest coal for me...
Once more, I saw her, as she started,
And glanced at me with red lips parted:

And, as she looked, the frightened hare
Had fled her eyes; and, merrily,
She smiled, with fine teeth flashing white,
As though she, too, were happy-hearted...
Then she had trembled suddenly,
And dropped her eyes, as that fat man
Stepped from the shadow of the van,
And joined the circle, as the pot
Was lifted off, and, piping-hot,
The supper steamed in wooden bowls.
Yet, she had hardly touched a bite:
And never raised her eyes all night
To mine again: but on the coals,
As I sat staring, she had stared--
The black curls, shining round her head
From under the red kerchief, tied
So nattily beneath her chin--
And she had stolen off to bed
Quite early, looking dazed and scared.
Then, all agape and sleepy-eyed,
Ere long the others had turned in:
And I was rid of that fat man,
Who slouched away to his own van.

And now, before her van, I lay,
With sleepless eyes, awaiting day:
And, as I gazed upon the glare,
I heard, behind, a gentle stir:
And, turning round, I looked on her
Where she stood on the little stair
Outside the van, with listening air--
And, in her eyes, the hunted hare...
And then, I saw her slip away,
A bundle underneath her arm,
Without a single glance at me.

I lay a moment wondering,
My heart a-thump like anything,
Then, fearing she should come to harm,
I rose, and followed speedily
Where she had vanished in the night.
And, as she heard my step behind,
She started, and stopt dead with fright:
Then blundered on as if struck blind:
And now as I caught up with her,
Just as she took the moorland track,
I saw the hare's eyes, big and black...
She made as though she'd double back...
But, when she looked into my eyes,
She stood quite still and did not stir...
And, picking up her fallen pack,
I tucked it 'neath my arm; and she
Just took her luck quite quietly,
As she must take what chance might come,
And would not have it otherwise,
And walked into the night with me,
Without a word across the fells.

And, all about us, through the night,
The mists were stealing, cold and white,
Down every rushy syke or slack:
But, soon the moon swung into sight:
And, as we went, my heart was light,
And singing like a burn in flood:
And in my ears were tinkling bells:
My body was a rattled drum:
And fifes were shrilling through my blood
That summer night, to think that she
Was walking through the world with me.

But when the air with dawn was chill,
As we were travelling down a hill,

She broke her silence with low-sobbing:
And told her tale, her bosom throbbing
As though her very heart were shaken
With fear she'd yet be overtaken...
She'd always lived in caravans--
Her father's, gay as any man's,
Grass-green, picked out with red and yellow
And glittering brave with burnished brass
That sparkled in the sun like flame,
And window curtains, white as snow...
But, they had died, ten years ago,
Her parents both, when fever came...
And they were buried, side by side,
Somewhere beneath the wayside grass...
In times of sickness, they kept wide
Of towns and busybodies, so
No parson's or policeman's tricks
Should bother them when in a fix...
Her father never could abide
A black coat or a blue, poor man...
And so, Long Dick, a kindly fellow,
When you could keep him from the can,
And Meg, his easy-going wife,
Had taken her into their van;
And kept her since her parents died...
And she had lived a happy life,
Until Fat Pete's young wife was taken...
But, ever since, he'd pestered her...
And she dared scarcely breathe or stir,
Lest she should see his eyes aleer...
And many a night she'd lain and shaken,
And very nearly died of fear--
Though safe enough within the van
With Mother Meg and her good-man--
For, since Fat Pete was Long Dick's friend,

And they were thick and sweet as honey;
And Dick owed Pete a pot of money,
She knew too well how it must end...
And she would rather lie stone dead
Beneath the wayside grass than wed
With leering Pete, and live the life,
And die the death, of his first wife...
And so, last night, clean-daft with dread,
She'd bundled up a pack and fled...

When all the sobbing tale was out,
She dried her eyes, and looked about,
As though she'd left all fear behind,
And out of sight were out of mind.
Then, when the dawn was burning red,
"I'm hungry as a hawk!" she said:
And from the bundle took out bread.
And, at the happy end of night,
We sat together by a burn:
And ate a thick slice, turn by turn;
And laughed and kissed between each bitc.

Then, up again, and on our way
We went; and tramped the livelong day
The moorland trackways, steep and rough,
Though there was little fear enough
That they would follow on our flight.

And then again a shiny night
Among the honey-scented heather,
We wandered in the moonblaze bright,
Together through a land of light,
A lad and lass alone with life.
And merrily we laughed together,
When, starting up from sleep, we heard
The cock-grouse talking to his wife...
And "Old Fat Pete" she called the bird.

Six months and more have cantered by:
And, Winter past, we're out again--
We've left the fat and weatherwise
To keep their coops and reeking sties,
And eat their fill of oven-pies,
While we win free and out again
To take potluck beneath the sky
With sun and moon and wind and rain.
Six happy months ... and yet, at night,
I've often wakened in affright,
And looked upon her lying there,
Beside me sleeping quietly,
Adread that when she waked, I'd see
The hunted hare within her eyes.

And, only last night, as I slept
Beneath the shelter of a stack...
My hands were hot upon a hare,
Half-strangled, struggling in the snare,
When, suddenly, her eyes shot back,
Big, fearful, staggering and black;
And ere I knew, my grip was slack,
And I was clutching empty air...
Bolt-upright from my sleep I leapt...
Her place was empty in the straw...
And then, with quaking heart, I saw
That she was standing in the night,
A leveret cuddled to her breast...

I spoke no word: but, as the light
Through banks of Eastern cloud was breaking,
She turned, and saw that I was waking:
And told me how she could not rest;
And, rising in the night, she'd found
This baby-hare crouched on the ground;
And she had nursed it quite a while:

But, now, she'd better let it go...
Its mother would be fretting so...
A mother's heart...
I saw her smile,
And look at me with tender eyes:
And as I looked into their light,
My foolish, fearful heart grew wise...
And now, I knew that never there
I'd see again the startled hare,
Or need to dread the dreams of night.
1910-1911.